David Watson

Evangelism, Renewal, Reconciliation

Matthew Porter

Vicar of St Chad's, Woodseats, Sheffield

GROVE BOOKS LIMITED
RIDLEY HALL RD   CAMBRIDGE   CB3 9HU

Contents

Acknowledgments

I am grateful to those who agreed to be interviewed in the course of my research into David Watson. Of those interviewed, the following have been quoted in this book:

Phil Clarke, Director of Evangelism, Methodist Church

John Collins, retired Vicar of Holy Trinity Brompton; Canford Magna; St Mark's Gillingham

Graham Cray, now Bishop of Maidstone; then Principal of Ridley Hall, Cambridge

Michael Green, evangelist and theologian

Nicky Gumbel, *Alpha* Chaplain and author

David Hilborn, Theological Advisor of Evangelical Alliance

Sue Hope, Diocesan Missioner for Diocese of Sheffield; then Vicar of St John the Baptist, Chapeltown, Sheffield

David MacInnes, then Vicar St Aldate's Oxford

Diana Nairne, then staff member St Aldate's Oxford; (ex-St Michael-le-Belfrey Team)

Martyn Percy, Director, Lincoln Theological Institute, Sheffield

Gavin Reid, then Bishop of Maidstone; previously Decade of Evangelism Adviser

Rob Warner, author; speaker; leader of *Kairos*, Wimbledon; ex-publisher with Hodder & Stoughton

Anne Watson, widow of David Watson

Murray Watts, playwright; founding member of Riding Lights Theatre Company

Gary Wilton, Director of Studies, Wilson Carlile College of Evangelism (Church Army)

Please note: non-referenced quotes come from taped interviews conducted during my research.

The Cover Illustration is by Peter Ashton

First Impression April 2003
ISSN 1470-8531
ISBN 1 85174 529 7

Introduction 1

In 1984 a fifty-year-old Anglican church leader died, after a year long battle against cancer.

Converted from atheism as an undergraduate, he made a huge impact on the church in the UK and beyond and particularly helped re-envision the evangelical and charismatic wings of the Church of England. His name was David Watson.

In the early 1990s Saunders and Samson wrote an excellent biography of Watson,[1] suggesting that his influence was still felt in the church. This was where my interest in Watson began. Were they right? What exactly were the themes of Watson's life and ministry? Does his legacy extend to the contemporary church? Are there lessons for us to learn from his life?

Having extensively investigated Watson, through reading his writings and books about him, listening to his teaching tapes, reading the teaching notes he intended using at Fuller Seminary in 1983, and especially through interviewing 17 people in 1999 for a contemporary perspective on the Watson legacy, here are some quotations unearthed through my research, commenting on the legacy of David Watson:

Leadership
- 'possibly the spiritual leader who in life and death has made the greatest impact on contemporary Christian life in Britain' (Peter Hocken, 1988).
- 'As the churches enter the Decade of Evangelism it may be that their capacity to do so owes more to David [Watson] than any other single person' (T Saunders and H Samson, 1992).

Charismatic Movement
- David Watson 'made the charismatic movement accessible to Anglicans' (Sue Hope, 1999).
- Watson 'gave permission for the next generation of church leaders to build charismatic evangelical churches' (Gary Wilton, 1999).
- 'the sane renewal leader' (Gavin Reid, 1999).

Evangelism
- Watson 'had an impact as evangelist and teacher second only to Billy Graham' (Michael Green, 1982).

- 'I don't think we could have done the Billy Graham projects in the '80s if it hadn't been for David Watson's ministry in the 1970s' (Gavin Reid, 1999).

Ecumenism
- Watson 'helped forward proper ecumenism more than perhaps anyone else in Britain during his life' (Michael Harper, 1985).

Arts
- 'I can't think of anyone who would…be as significant a figure in the Christian arts during my life' (Murray Watts, 1999).

Worship: Songs and Multimedia
- 'St Michael's was paving the way for a new style of simple worship songs in the UK church' (Graham Cray, 1999).
- 'the visuals that were banners [at St Michael-le-Belfrey] became the visuals that are electronic screens' (Graham Cray, 1999).

Who was this man? What was his background? What motivated him? For those with little or no knowledge of Watson a biographical sketch may be useful.

2 Biographical Sketch

1933–59

David Christopher Knight Watson was born on 7th March 1933. His father, a Christian Scientist, died a month before Watson's tenth birthday after refusing treatment for bronchial pneumonia. David Watson was educated at Wellington College where he was an able sportsman and became Head of School. After National Service in the Royal Artillery he went up to St John's College, Cambridge in October 1954, where he had been awarded an Exhibition. During 'Freshers Week' he attended a talk by John Collins, a Curate from All Souls,' Langham Place and as a result was converted to Christianity, having decided at school that he was an atheist.

Watson's faith was nurtured in those early days by the evangelical CICCU (Cambridge Inter-Collegiate Christian Union), by the England cricketer David

Sheppard and by fellow student David MacInnes. He began attending Bash Camps,[2] changed his degree from Philosophy to Theology, was accepted for ordination in the Church of England and completed his theological training at Ridley Hall, Cambridge.

1959–65

David Watson was ordained deacon in September 1959 (and presbyter/priest in 1960) and was Curate, with David MacInnes, under his mentor John Collins[3] at St Mark's, Gillingham. All three have had influential evangelistic ministries within the Church of England. Gillingham was a most formative period where the foundational skills of Watson's future ministry were laid.

In September 1962 he moved to a second curacy at 'The Round Church' in Cambridge where he was able to develop his evangelistic gifts amongst the students. David MacInnes recalled that Watson 'was asked to do two CICCU missions in succession, which for a person resident in Cambridge was absolutely unheard of.' Soon after moving to Cambridge Watson experienced what is now described as 'charismatic renewal.'[4] This affected every aspect of his future ministry and Watson soon became known not just as a good evangelist but also a renewal preacher.

In September 1964 Watson married Anne MacEwan Smith. Watson openly admitted that their personalities and gifts meant that marriage was hard but rewarding. Their children Fiona and Guy were born in 1966 and 1969 respectively.

1965–81

July 1965 saw the Watsons move to York where they took on St Cuthbert's— a church planned for redundancy. It was soon full and in January 1973 the congregation moved to the larger building of St Michael-le-Belfrey next to York Minster. The church became known as a centre of evangelism and renewal with particular emphasis on relationships and the use of the arts in worship and mission. St Michael-le-Belfrey developed a number of community households and held 'renewal weeks' to encourage other churches and their leaders.

David Watson's evangelistic gifts took him to many universities and towns in the UK and abroad. He travelled with a team of musicians and artists who sought to proclaim the gospel through their presentations and their lifestyle.

In the early 1970s Watson realized that reconciliation between Christians was crucial for the church to be effective in its life and mission. Thus by the mid-1970s what Graham Cray describes as 'the mature Watson vision' of *evangelism, renewal* and *reconciliation* was firmly established. This study is shaped by these three themes of Watson's ministry.

He also developed a significant writing ministry. His sermons were recorded and available to the Christian public and just before his death in the early days of video he helped write and present an evangelistic video course— *Jesus Then and Now.*

1981-84

In 1981 he met and became friends with John Wimber, an American known then as a church growth expert. Wimber's ministry deeply affected Watson— particularly the remarkable healings he saw while visiting Wimber's Anaheim Vineyard Church. Wimber visited York that summer which marked the beginning of Wimber's influential UK ministry during the 1980s and early 1990s.

The family moved to London in August 1982 to launch a new phase of Watson's national and international ministry although this was cut short by cancer surgery in January 1983. The surgery was successful although revealed inoperable secondaries in the liver. Watson was given about a year to live.

Many Christians, including John Wimber, prayed for Watson's physical healing. Watson himself described the experience:

> I felt a tremendous surge of heat as well as vibrations in my body, and I knew that God was at work. This went on for half an hour or more, and we all had no doubt that God was with us. 'That was quite a time!' said John Wimber (as indeed it was).[5]

Wimber believed Watson would be healed although never explicitly said he *would* be healed. For the sceptics, Watson's illness became a test case for the charismatic healing ministry. David Watson died on 18th February 1984, a few weeks before his 51st birthday.

Despite Watson's death, Wimber's ministry took off in the UK. Much of this was a result of Watson's endorsement of Wimber, especially in his many references to him in his book, *Fear No Evil*, published a few months after his death in 1984.

Fear No Evil was his final book and demonstrated Watson's commitment to mission and evangelism. In it he described the reality of living with cancer and how this affected his faith, his family and his theology of healing. The book encouraged and challenged both the Christian and the unbeliever about the realities of suffering, life and death.

In the next chapter I therefore begin the analysis of Watson by examining this passion for mission and evangelism.

Evangelism

3

After his conversion, Watson was well schooled in evangelism, especially through the CICCU, Bash and John Collins and was soon recognized as having an evangelistic gift.

Michael Green, one of the Church of England's most effective evangelistic communicators over the last three or four decades, told me that to be a good evangelist 'you need to engage the feelings; you need to capture the intellect; you need to get to the will—that's the critical thing.' Watson did all these and more, so much so that Green would not accept that Watson was just a good evangelist—for Green, 'he was a *brilliant* evangelist.' Furthermore Watson was able to communicate in this way in both the personal, small-group and the large audience setting.

Evangelism and Mission

Watson believed that evangelism—the task of proclaiming the good news of Christ—was fundamental to the life of the church. In fact, the church engaged in mission, because 'God is a missionary. His redemptive work in the world is missionary work.'[6] Watson expresses here the *missio dei*—the idea that God has a mission to the world with which Christians join when they carry out the church's mission. For Watson, Christian mission therefore is to be set within the framework of God and his kingdom, for 'the aim of missionary work is not just to win individuals for Christ; it is to extend the kingdom of God.'[7]

> *For Watson, Christian mission is to be set within the framework of God and his kingdom*

He supported the Lausanne Covenant—the result of a 1974 congress on world evangelization—affirming that 'although evangelism and social action are distinct, both are vitally and equally important in the total mission of the church.'[8] His passion for Christian social action was seen in his commitment to 'simple lifestyle' Christianity and practical care for the poor and oppressed. Sue Hope thinks Watson influenced Wimber in this, which may explain something of the Vineyard movement's concern for the disadvantaged since the

1980s. Caring for the poor is still a strong emphasis in the contemporary Vineyard movement. Watson's influence here has not, to date, been recognized.

In the wider contemporary church most leaders from across the theological spectrum would agree with Watson, that evangelism is part of mission rather than mission in totality. After John Stott, Watson was one of the first conservative evangelical Anglicans to articulate this—perhaps *the* first at a popular level. Any continued influence in this area today is mainly through his writing, the legacy of his preaching and teaching and the kind of church he sought to grow, because for Watson the local church in the local context was crucial for effective mission and evangelism.

Evangelism and Local Context

At St Cuthbert's and St Michael-le-Belfrey Watson sought to build a radical, relevant church. Hence Michael Green felt that Watson was the right person to write the book *I Believe in the Church*—the ecclesiological work of the popular 'I Believe' series. Although he travelled widely, Watson knew the importance of the *local* church:

> In many ways church missions and evangelistic crusades are God's second-best: if every local church was truly alive with the Spirit of God there would be no need for the considerable time, money and energy expended on these special events.[9]

Today's thinking on evangelism by mission consultants such as Robert Warren likewise questions the priority of *the evangelist* and talks of the importance of *the church member* and *the church itself* as 'the primary agent of mission.'[10] There has been an increasing trend away from large-scale evangelistic events and a greater emphasis placed on local church mission. Nevertheless, Bishop Gavin Reid—who organized Billy Graham's UK evangelistic efforts in the 1980s—felt that Watson's role in the evangelical church in the 1970s was crucial as preparation for the large-scale events of the 1980s:

> I really *do* want to stress that actually evangelicals were losing the plot in the 1970s…We were getting involved in so many important things…[but] the thing that we were supposed to do best we were doing less of! And of course it was getting more difficult. But to his credit, David never lost the plot. Now when David died, who were the people we picked up to get behind Billy [Graham]? They were the people who'd worked with David. I don't think we could have done the Billy projects in the '80s if it hadn't been for David Watson's ministry in the 1970s.

For evangelism to be effective *today* many feel there needs to be a re-working of its very nature—a shift from maintenance to mission—and the building of missionary congregations.

St Michael-le-Belfrey was a model of a church experiencing both spiritual growth (renewal) *and* numerical growth—mainly through its evangelistic witness. It cannot be overstated how important this was, at a time when large numbers of people were leaving the church—especially the Church of England.[11] Church authorities were understandably encouraged by St Michael's, as were clergy and other church leaders. There are many leaders in the church today whose concern for church-based evangelism was inspired by St Michael-le-Belfrey and the way in which Watson took notice of the culture of his day.

Evangelism and Cultural Context

Watson believed that Christians needed to take their cultural context seriously, living and speaking in a way that resonated with people's lives. He sought to model this himself, especially in his preaching. He wrote:

> What was relevant yesterday may be quite irrelevant today. Although the essential gospel never changes, the manner in which it is proclaimed and demonstrated must reveal the fact that we are dealing with the God of today. It is only when people hear his voice today that we can urge them, in the name of Christ, not to harden their hearts but to turn to him in repentance and faith.[12]

Watson felt that the church should be answering the questions people have, and addressing people's 'felt moods.' The evangelist therefore had to try to get into the minds of his audience.

This is a view shared today by many Anglican evangelicals. Interestingly, one of the Church of England's experts on contemporary evangelistic communication is Graham Cray, who was highly influenced by Watson, working under him at St Michael's and then becoming Vicar after him in 1982. Cray, now Bishop of Maidstone, has written and taught extensively on the cultural shift that has taken place in the West in recent years. Sociologists describe this as a shift from modernity to postmodernity, where modernity represents the Enlightenment worldview, and postmodernity a reaction against the thinking of modernity. According to Cray,

> ...we were not into anything that was dominantly post-modern before the 1980s. But clearly the writing was on the wall.

Watson was able to read the signs of the times and so, says Cray, his communication reflected

> the need to be visual and not just verbal; the need for experience; the breaking away from a purely linear, rational way of thinking. Now David was very linear and rational, but my goodness, was there a lot of stuff going on to break it up and make it accessible!

Watson was aware of the beginnings of this cultural shift partly through his involvement with the arts and his sponsoring of *The Riding Lights Theatre Company*. *Riding Lights* became probably the best known Christian theatre company in the nation—mainly due to Watson's influence. His encouraging of the creative arts was radical for the time as many still saw this as an ungodly arena. Watson, however, realized the value of the arts for worship and evangelism.

Murray Watts was a founding member of *Riding Lights* and is now a leading Christian playwright. He thinks that

> David single-handedly re-awoke the idea of the church as patron of the theatre.

Watson's influence in this field is rarely noted.

Watts and his colleague Paul Burbridge found, with Watson, much theological inspiration in a Dutch professor of arts, Hans Rookmaaker, and particularly in his *Modern Art and the Death of a Culture* (1970).[13] Rookmaaker's prophetic thesis was that the western world was going through 'a great cultural revolution.' He writes of the Enlightenment changing the world and being 'the period in which we today are still living, though at its end. Its aims have been fulfilled. The world is different.'[14]

Watson tried to use methods and media that communicated effectively with the people of his day—a people 'starved of love, suffocated with words, bereft of joy and lacking in peace.'[15] David Bebbington devotes significant space in his *Evangelicalism in Modern Britain* to the way in which the style and spirituality of 1970s charismatic evangelicalism attempted to speak to its culture. The picture he paints describes, almost perfectly—and perhaps purposefully—St Michael-le-Belfrey:

> The whole movement released a surge of creativity that included making banners, designing graphics, writing songs, playing instruments, moulding pottery and performing sacred dance. Craft and coffee shops became a charismatic cottage industry. Technical skills found an outlet in operating grand public address systems and the humble overhead projectors that permitted congregations to worship unencumbered with hymn books. Drama, far from being condemned, was harnessed to Christian purposes, with acted presentations in worship, mime in the streets and evangelistic puppet shows. David

> Watson's congregation generated a full-time theatre company, Riding Lights. There was an extraordinarily unevangelical delight in symbol—'a love of oil, candles, crosses, etc.' The resulting artistic effervescence was very reasonably labelled 'inchoate sacramentality.' 'Verbal communication,' a charismatic folk arts handbook declared, is 'clumsy and wearying.'[16]

For Bebbington, the whole evangelical movement—of which charismatic spirituality is a part—is a product of, and rooted in, a modernist, Enlightenment worldview. I disagree with this, and prefer the view of Cray:

> I don't think [Watson] was wedded to a certain era of charismatic worship, dance, banners and drama. I think he was wedded to what will communicate.

I went on to ask Graham Cray where he now saw Watson in terms of gospel and culture. His view is that Watson

> was one of the bridge people, because he was implying, 'we cannot do things the way we used to.' He opened people up for that sort of debate that was to follow.

That debate is still taking place, alongside a degree of consensus that the nature and style of the local church affects the relevance of evangelism today.

It is also increasingly recognized that becoming a Christian is a process rather than an event.[17] The key question for the evangelist today then, is not necessarily whether they have helped someone make a Christian commitment, but whether they have helped them progress on the journey to faith. In reality, this process of evangelism has been recognized for some time. The Engel Scale—which Watson used—is an example of an evangelistic tool which recognizes that people do not normally turn from unbelief to belief without some prior Christian influence.[18]

Watson therefore worked hard at speaking people's language, and the main context he found to do this was in St Michael's guest services.

Evangelism and Local Church Models

St Michael-le-Belfrey had quite a name in the 1970s for its 'guest services'—many of which took place in York Minster. These were evangelistic services to which Christians could bring their friends and family in order to hear a stirring, contemporary message about following Christ. Central to the service was the verbal evangelistic challenge, which Watson had learned from John Collins (at Gillingham) and Collins had learned from John Stott (at All

Souls). Watson, however, added music and drama and included *worship* as a key component in his services. This became known as 'celebration evangelism.'

These services led many people to faith in Jesus Christ—people whose subsequent influence on the church and world is difficult to quantify. Just as difficult to measure is the positive psychological effect that these successful evangelistic endeavours had on the shrinking church, reminding people that conversion to the Christian faith still took place. The 'celebration evangelism' model also went on to prepare the UK church for the 'power evangelism' expounded by John Wimber in the 1980s—where enthusiastic worship and signs and wonders were claimed to help people find faith in Christ.

Evangelicals who later struggled with the theology of 'power evangelism' often supported 'seeker services' developed in the late 1980s, a model of evangelism associated with Willow Creek Community Church in Chicago, and still popular today. Seeker services are gospel presentations, not worship. Whilst Watson would no doubt have struggled with the idea of excluding worship from evangelistic events, Rob Warner told me that Watson's and St Michael's clear communication and extensive use of the creative arts prepared the UK church for this kind of 'seeker-friendly' evangelism.

A significant model of evangelism popular in the UK since the mid-1990s is *Alpha*. *Alpha* has been developed by Nicky Gumbel of Holy Trinity Brompton into one of the most effective evangelistic initiatives in recent times. It is a mix of both the 'seeker service' and 'power evangelism' models. The church in the UK was prepared for both these models by Watson. But Watson's influence on Alpha may go beyond its style—he might even have affected its content. Watson's books and *Alpha's* course-book *Questions of Life* share some material.[19] This, of course, should not be surprising as Watson was one of the clearest evangelistic communicators of his generation, and material is often shared across the church in this way. However, the link with John Collins is probably crucial here, as Nicky Gumbel told me that:

> A lot of David Watson's illustrations originally came from John Collins and…a huge amount of the *Alpha* material came from John Collins. For example, the Holy Spirit weekend was all from John Collins, and he had a huge input into the original *Alpha* course, which John Irvine produced under him. So John is the link.

John Collins' influence on *Alpha* has never been properly recognized.

David Watson's evangelistic legacy therefore extends, indirectly and directly, even to the contemporary *Alpha* course. *Alpha* and charismatic evangelicals represent a stream within the church that has always longed for effective evangelism to develop into Holy Spirit revival—a desire shared by Watson.

Evangelism and Revival

In his Fuller notes, Watson claims to cite John Stott in saying:

> The desperate need of the church today is the Holy Spirit. We need individual Christians to be filled with the Holy Spirit. More than that, we need revival, a mighty supernatural visitation of the Holy Spirit in the community.

Watson distinguished between the *renewal* of the church and *revival*, which is this sovereign work of the Spirit that spills out into the world and results in a significant evangelistic harvest. According to David MacInnes, revival

> …was a big topic that was with us since the 60s…Somewhere I've got notes of a talk that David gave in which he was spelling out all the signs of the times and the likelihood of God breaking in in some way. So I think although he didn't write about [revival] a great deal, it was a continual theme.

MacInnes went on to talk of how Watson often spoke of the Hebridean revival in his talks. Watson believed that St Michael's was seeing something of this at a local level in the charismatic renewal. Cray thinks this

> awoke in him a longing that something similar should happen but which involved the conviction and conversion of people outside church…I think it was the combination of the evangelist in him and the person committed to and called to renewal that therefore had a longing and an appetite for revival.

The hope of revival today is still strong in many quarters of evangelicalism. Watson has had little direct influence on that expectation—and quotations from Watson are not normally cited by those encouraging revival today. However, Watson did not hold back from communicating his clear conviction that God wanted to renew his church in preparation for revival—and that at St Michael-le-Belfrey and elsewhere, he was beginning to do that. He wrote:

> how many seriously long for and pray for a powerful spiritual renewal or revival? How many understand that only this will save the church from death and the world from disaster?[20]

For David Watson, revival could not be achieved simply through evangelism—which has been the theme of this chapter. Indeed he thought that there could be no revival without a renewed church, and it is to that issue that we turn.

4 Renewal

These days 'renewal' is a fairly broad term which I define as a reawakening of love for God brought about by his Spirit.

In 1970 'renewal' meant charismatic renewal, which brought much of the theology and practice of Pentecostalism into the mainline churches. For many, Watson seemed to epitomize all that was good about renewal.

Renewed People

Watson modelled this renewal through his church in York. The church became probably the best-known 'renewed' Anglican church in the country. Even John Collins, whose influence on the Church of England has been immense, admitted

> I can't imagine how I could have got on without David doing what he did in York. He had a profound influence...I *do* believe that the beacon of light that he lit at St Michael's, York really enabled the whole movement of the Spirit to survive, and that has had a profound influence...

Of course, St Michael-le-Belfrey was not the only church experiencing charismatic renewal, but nevertheless its influence at the time encouraged other churches and their leaders. This was summed up for me by Gary Wilton. For him, Watson and St Michael's were an inspiration, which

> gave permission for the next generation of church leaders to build charismatic evangelical churches.

The impact of St Michael-le-Belfrey as a model of a local church in renewal is no doubt still felt today in thousands of individuals and hundreds of churches, including St Aldate's, Oxford and St Thomas', Lancaster—to name but two that have emerged through my research. In reality, the wider influence of a church like St Michael's is impossible to quantify.

But what was it that was attractive about St Michael-le-Belfrey? According to Graham Cray:

> the prime value of St Cuthbert's and St Michael-le-Belfrey was the quality of relationships that come from being reconciled to Christ.

For some, this was worked out in various community households—homes with joint possessions and communal incomes. Sue Hope lived with the Watson family in one of these houses in York and I asked her whether there might still be a place for such households. Her response was affirmative—she thinks they are still 'a charism of the church.' The community households, however, were not without their tensions and only lasted a few years—a great disappointment to David and Anne Watson. The verdict given by many of my interviewees was that the Watsons nobly experimented with this idea that might yet have its time again.

Renewal at St Michael-le-Belfrey therefore brought a strong emphasis on *people* and *relationships*. Indeed, renewed worshippers were more important than renewed worship.

Renewed Worship

When people experienced the worship, what did they discover? According to Cray, they:

> found a group of people who quite clearly believed what they were singing and praying, and interpreted what was going on as the fact that they were actually encountering the God they were worshipping.

In this expectant, worshipping atmosphere the services were creative, colourful and vibrant. There was dance, drama, banners and contemporary music. Such things were not common in the Anglican church at that time. To a large extent St Michael's pioneered this in the UK, although they were greatly influenced, especially musically, by The Church of the Redeemer in Houston and their Fisherfolk. St Michael's role was to contextualize the style for the UK scene.

There are, then, links between the creative and artistic expressions at St Michael's and modern worship today. This link is probably most pronounced in the area of contemporary worship *music*, for it was David Watson—through his missions and his church—who was the most significant force introducing this 'folk song' style of worship to the British church scene in the 1970s.

These songs have since developed into a whole new genre, known as 'worship songs' which are now common in much of the church—especially evangelical Anglican churches in the UK. Both Graham Cray and Michael Green recognize the influence of St Michael's on the music and worship of the wider church. According to Green, this kind of simple musical style has

> become very normative, and the songs from those days are either still in existence—lots of them—or they have spawned a new generation of the same sort of thing.

Watson's important role in establishing this kind of music has not been noted to date. The 'alternative worship' stream, that developed through the 1980s and 90s—and is a growing style of worship for young people today—was also highly influenced by Watson.

Alternative worship gained notoriety in 1995 when the leader of the leading alternative worship service—The 9 O'clock Service (NOS) in Sheffield—was exposed for sexual impropriety and abusive relationships. Nevertheless, NOS did set the tone for this new movement. Graham Cray told me that

> David Watson and St Michael's were really important to [NOS]…They would regularly come and be at the services. And David was very significant for them and in a sense what they did with video and house music was to take the same principles and apply them to the forms of art and communication of club culture. So it's a direct knock on, in which case, what David and St Michael's did is one of the tributaries of the whole alternative worship thing—using a different medium.

In the 1980s the strongest influence on mainline UK renewal music was the American Vineyard churches. However, even this had Watson's hand on it, for, according to Graham Cray:

> We engaged with Wimber on worship because the way had been prepared for us through [Watson's] 'celebration evangelism' approach.

Renewal, however, was about more than music—it was about the presence of the Spirit available today to transform, empower and equip. Watson's clear thinking made him a practical theologian of this charismatic renewal.

Renewed Theology

Watson was not an academic theologian, but he had a sharp mind and was able to articulate a compelling and attractive case placing the charismatic experience soundly within the context of Scripture—despite the opposition of many conservative evangelicals to the charismatic movement in the 1960s.[21] Michael Green remembers that

> …he got people to see that the word of God is alive and that the Spirit and the word are friends and not foes. And so he neither had an arid intellectualism on Scripture nor did he have a goofy emotionalism with the Spirit. The two kept in step with one another.

His evangelical background had birthed in Watson a conservative view of Scripture but his reading and experience enabled him to see the inadequacy of literal or anti-intellectual approaches to the Bible. Phil Clarke found him helpful on this:

> His style indicates that he has a high view of the authority of Scripture without coming across as an unthinking fundamentalist. I think we can learn a lot from that. He believes the Bible and he puts it into action, he puts it to work. He works on the assumption that this is God's message.

Watson's experience of the Holy Spirit's renewing power in the early 1960s came, to a large extent, out of reading the Bible and the experience transformed his own life and ministry. He wrote: 'I was in love with Jesus in a way I had never known before' and then describes how his Bible reading, praise, prayer, personal evangelism and love for people were heightened.[22]

The evangelist now had a message for Christians, although he needed to understand it more deeply and intellectually. He wrote in his autobiography:

> But what exactly *had* God done in my life? The reality of it all was unmistakable and undeniable, but how could I understand it in biblical and theological terms? That was the difficulty. So began six months or more of furious study to try to grasp from the Scriptures what it was all about.[23]

His book *One in the Spirit* (1973) reflects this attempt to marry the word and the Spirit by saying that all Christians are baptized in the Spirit in status, but not necessarily in experience. This kind of pneumatology, even though articulated at a popular level, was progressive in that it was not enunciated so clearly until the so-called 'Third Wave' theology of the early 1980s.[24]

Renewed Power

The term 'Third Wave' has never caught on in the UK, although most evangelicals have heard of its most influential practitioner—John Wimber—and his books *Power Evangelism* and *Power Healing*.[25] Watson and Wimber became close friends for the last three years of Watson's life and Wimber subsequently went on to have a dominant influence over charismatic renewal in the Church of England and beyond during the 1980s and early 1990s. If David Watson was 'Mr Renewal' of the 1970s, John Wimber took up the mantle in the 1980s.

In terms of personality, temperament, background, gifting, style, dress and manner, the two were poles apart. Watson was the understated, eloquent, public school educated Englishman. Wimber was the laid-back, open-shirted Californian who often described himself as 'just a fat man trying to get to heaven.' Their friendship has intrigued many, but more importantly for the life of the future church, Watson opened the door to Wimber in the UK, a man who has had significant influence on parts of the Church of England.

Apart from becoming great friends, there are two further reasons for the Watson-Wimber partnership—one theological and the other pragmatic.

Although Watson was trained as an Anglican priest and Wimber a Quaker minister, by 1981 their theological journeys had to a large extent converged and they found they had much in common. They both led seemingly successful churches, were committed to church growth, encouraged home groups, desired more of the Spirit's power, had a conservative view of Scripture, and saw 'the kingdom of God' as the key theme around which all renewal ministry should be practised.

Pragmatically, their friendship met needs in both. Wimber, for instance, needed Watson as a way into the UK. Wimber told a 1994 Conference in London that in 1968 he

> came for the first time to London and walked the streets, looking for revival. God had given me a vision that revival was going to come and hit this country and through this country go to Germany and then all over Europe…I believe that God will use this nation, coupled with Germany to take revivals to the ends of the earth. I've believed that now since 1968…I've always believed it. I believe that's what my life is all about—is to see that happen. [26]

Watson needed Wimber and 'power evangelism' to counter his insecurity and renew his vision for a new phase of ministry. Martyn Percy suspects in Watson

> a certain amount of cognitive dissonance at work—certainly a slight feeling of disillusionment and I think Wimber filled an important gap and presented a viable way forward for the programme of evangelical revivalism that he presented.

By January 1981, Watson was at the height of his power. It was a well-established joke that he 'was leading the Church of England from York' but he was unsettled and his meeting with Wimber caused another revolution in his life and ministry.

Anne Watson described five effects of meeting Wimber. First, there was 'a paradigm shift in relationships' for David. She told me that

> John Wimber just *liked* David, and that was unusual for him, because most of his life he earned everything…It's something I'd prayed for for years, that David would find somebody who just liked him for who he was, because I don't think he'd ever really known that.

Secondly, he saw and participated in healing miracles to a degree that he had never experienced before. Thirdly, Watson saw that effective ministry was not dependent on godliness. Anne told me that her husband

> had been living good all his life. Good at everything. He'd never stepped out of line. But Wimber, you know? Drinking coke. Eating chips. Laughing. And then ten words of knowledge would come!

Fourthly, it re-stimulated his theological thinking. Anne also said

> I remember going out to stay with Carol and John [Wimber]. I'd never seen David like that before. They had all these heated talks—all sorts of theological discussions!

Fifthly, her husband discovered from Wimber that ministry could be fun. Wimber had a good sense of humour, was not afraid to hold staff meetings on the beach and sincerely enjoyed ministry in the power of the Spirit. This was compelling to David Watson.

Wimber was invited to visit York in May 1981—that British trip being the start of Wimber's influential British ministry.[27] Ironically it was during and through Watson's subsequent cancer diagnosis and eventual death that the profile of this 'healing evangelist' was raised in the UK—and this was mainly due to Watson's endorsement of Wimber.

Wimber has been widely criticized inside and outside evangelicalism, both during his ministry and since his death in 1997. The main controversy relates to his 'power evangelism' thesis, that the proclamation of the gospel accompanied with signs and wonders will produce large numbers of converts. Those who consider Wimber's ministry to have been unhelpful for charismatic renewal and for evangelicalism in general find it difficult that Watson—the man described by Gavin Reid as 'the sane renewal leader'—should be responsible for Wimber's introduction to the UK. What they fail to realize, however, is the extent of the change that took place in Watson in 1981.

The catalyst for this 'paradigm shift' was his experience of meeting Wimber and visiting the Anaheim Vineyard in January 1981. Wimber, speaking some fourteen years after this visit recalled:

> At one point David Watson was following me around watching people getting healed and he said to me, 'How do you do that?' and I said, 'Oh, easy!' and I said, 'Give me your hand' and I put it on a woman's eye that was blind and she saw, and David walked around like this, staring at his hand. (*Laughter*). He said, 'I did that! I did that! I participated in that!' and I said, 'Sure. What are they for if they're not for laying on people?' And he said, 'You make it look so easy' and I said, 'I don't make it look easy; *He* makes it look easy. What do you want me to do—try to pretend that it's hard? It's not hard; it's *impossible!!!*' These fat little freckled hands can't make something well.[28]

Anne Watson confirmed Wimber's description by saying,

> Oh yes. And he was actually doing it…and he just jumped into it. He was thrilled by it. I couldn't believe it, because he would never lift his hands when he was in worship. He spoke in tongues but nobody was ever told; he kept his hands under the hymn book. He was very reticent to be seen. But after this…he was dancing around—he was just a different person.

This meeting with Wimber precipitated significant changes in his life. By the summer Watson had decided on, although not publically announced, the move to London. It was a bold decision to leave a seemingly successful church and begin a whole new ministry (without a church) in London. What was he planning? Not surprisingly he was hoping to write and do more festivals and missions. What is not so well-known is that he was hoping to start a (probably non-denominational) theological seminary in the style of Fuller, in London. He also wanted to begin a new church targetting young people and based in an old theatre or disused cinema. This was similar to the model Wimber had employed in establishing the Anaheim Vineyard—showing the extent of Wimber's influence over Watson at this time. If these ventures had been successful he may well have left, or been forced to leave, the Church of England.

None of this happened, for the cancer took over and Watson died in February 1984, remembered for his profound and highly influential ministry, but with any difficulties and frustrations he had with the Anglican church—perhaps rightly—papered over for fear of unnecessary embarrassment.

Renewed Evangelicalism

David Watson died an Anglican—an evangelical Anglican—yet one who was able to transcend church tradition more than most. John Collins told me that in his missions Watson

> had this amazing ability—which I've never quite understood how he could hold together—a spectrum of Plymouth Brethren on the one hand and hold their confidence, and Roman Catholics on the other.

On his death-bed he was visited by the Bishop of London and also the Archbishop of Canterbury, the latter of whom said, 'I just want to thank him for all he has done for faith among God's people.' Archbishop Blanche of York had also recognized Watson's services to the worldwide church and within the Diocese of York when he moved to London, by making Watson a Canon Provincial of the Northern Province.

St Michael-le-Belfrey—the church Watson left behind—was one of the Church of England's 'success stories.' It was, however, no ordinary Anglican church. Both St Michael's and St Cuthbert's were what today would be called 'church plants.' At St Cuthbert's Watson was given free reign to build a whole new church, swallowing up the existing handful of believers. At St Michael's, the now large congregation of St Cuthbert's did a similar thing, taking on St Michael's building and incorporating their existing congregation into the 'new' St Michael's.

The kind of spirituality developed there was what Rob Warner has called 'a non-denominational evangelicalism,' which from time to time was at odds with the style of much of Anglicanism. The publication of an Archbishop's Council on Evangelism report on St Michael's in November 1977 recommended that the church become more Anglican in flavour. Warner thinks the report was 'a shot across the bows' by the Anglican authorities, as they:

> were never quite sure at that stage how much space to give David and how much to bounce him into touch.

Anne Watson also talked about tensions with the diocese and Church of England. She admitted that there were problems surfacing in the early 1980s:

> If he hadn't died, there'd have been a crisis. The crisis would have been: could he stay in the Church of England?

If Watson was sincere about developing a new young people's church in London there would have been a major clash between him and the Diocesan authorities, for the parish system in the Church of England does not allow clergy to start a new church wherever they wish. In the end it would have come down to this: the Church of England would either have had to relax their rules on parochial boundaries or be prepared to lose its leading evangelist and one of its most influential clergymen.[29] If Watson had then left Anglicanism it is highly likely that other evangelical clergy and their congregations would have joined him and the schism that Anglican evangelicals such as John Stott had worked so hard to forestall at the 1966 Second National Assembly of Evangelicals might in fact have taken place.

When I pressed Anne on this she felt that things would have become awkward if Wimber had started Vineyard churches in the UK while Watson was still alive. This is unlikely because Wimber had promised Watson that he would not start any UK Vineyard churches. Cray told me that Wimber did not see the need because of the high calibre of leadership in the Anglican church. Anne Watson said that Wimber changed his mind in the latter half of the 1980s. At the time of writing there are now 70 Vineyard churches in the UK and Ireland.

Some of my interviewees, such as Martyn Percy, hypothesized about Watson heading up the Vineyard in the UK, which would have been unlikely for two reasons. First, Watson was negative about 'house churches' that split from existing congregations, partly because of his experience in 1980 when a group broke away from St Michael's. Secondly, the move to London was to facilitate the broadening of Watson's influence. Heading up Vineyard UK may well have been too small a job. Nevertheless, Percy's suggestion, whilst being unlikely, is not impossible.

The scenario of Watson ministering as an independent evangelical would surely have increased the move to a more post-denominational evangelicalism. Since Watson's death there has still been an increasing trend towards post-denominationalism within the evangelical constituency—partly due to annual evangelical events such as *Spring Harvest* and the unifying role played by the Evangelical Alliance especially from the 1980s. There are now countless churches—especially Anglican churches—up and down the land where people's allegiance has more to do with the evangelical theology and style than denominational badge. There are also a number of independent evangelical churches that are first and foremost *evangelical,* and other issues are secondary. The Vineyard churches in the UK are a case in point. Whether this trend continues remains to be seen.

But how significant was St Michael's in taking evangelicalism to where it is today in the Church of England? It seems that St Michael's was an important church that modelled an early form of implicit post-denominational evangelicalism for the wider church. Its role here should not be *over*stated and yet in the 1970s (according to Warner) 'St Mike's was ahead of the game and it's become more normative since.' This move towards post-denominationalism amongst evangelicals remains a challenge to the contemporary Church of England. There are some signs that the Anglican church is recognizing this, as seen in its revised Electoral Roll forms, which now recognize those who regularly attend an Anglican church but were confirmed in or are members of other denominations. If the Church of England cannot accommodate this kind of ecclesiology there is surely a risk of future fragmentation.

In sum, Watson's influence in terms of the *renewal* of the Church of England was immense and can still be felt today—partly by his books, partly through renewal music and alternative worship, partly by his influence on individuals and churches (not the least St Michael's, which is still a significant church in the UK) and partly through the Wimber/Vineyard stream.

But renewal on its own was not sufficient to produce the kind of church Watson was looking for. Watson soon came to see that there could be no proper renewal without church unity and reconciliation.

Reconciliation 5

Christian reconciliation became such an important theme of David Watson's ministry that Michael Harper chose to dedicate a whole chapter to Watson 'The Reconciler' in A Portrait By His Friends.

Harper wrote:

> I believe that David's ministry helped forward proper ecumenism more than perhaps anyone else in Britain during that time.[30]

Reconciliation within Evangelicalism

From the early days of his charismatic experience Watson realized that unity amongst believers was important yet often difficult—it had to be modelled. He therefore appointed Andrew Cornes as his first curate. Watson wrote that whilst Cornes had an

> astute mind, obvious drive [and] gifts of leadership...one particular problem, however, had to be worked through with honesty. Andrew could not identify with the charismatic renewal, as it was now commonly called. However, my burden was already growing for the reconciling of Christians over this issue; and since Andrew's teaching was crystal clear about the heart of the biblical gospel which I constantly sought to proclaim, I felt that it might be good deliberately to invite, as curate, someone who was definitely not a 'card-carrying charismatic,' partly to demonstrate that our unity is always in Christ, and not in any particular spiritual experience.[31]

This issue has not disappeared from today's church. Arguably the biggest divide between Anglican evangelicals is still the charismatic/non-charismatic issue. Wimber's 'power evangelism' in the 1980s and the so-called 'Toronto Blessing' of the 1990s[32] in many ways re-defined the divide as evangelicals felt forced to choose whether or not to follow the latest new wave of charismatic interest.

Charismatic evangelicals today—both inside and outside the Church of England—tend to fall into two camps: (i) those who see the charismatic experience as a crucial extra component which marks them out from other evangelicals, and (ii) those who view their experience of the Spirit as part of and within the boundaries of evangelical orthodoxy. Watson was clearly part of the latter group, who find unity with other evangelicals easier than the former.

The question of whether charismatic/Pentecostal spirituality is a separate tradition within the life of the church is still a matter of debate. Nevertheless, Watson's influence as a bridge between charismatic and non-charismatic evangelicals in the Church of England was crucial and is still felt today by those who desire a greater integration of word and Spirit.

Reconciliation across Traditions

This reconciliation, however, was not confined to evangelicalism. In his autobiography, Watson describes his city-wide festivals and writes:

> Our overall aim is three-fold: reconciliation, renewal and evangelism. As far as *reconciliation* is concerned, it is thrilling to see Christians of all traditions come together, usually with few exceptions, and discover one another in Christ.[33]

Watson wrote openly about the difficulties he had in acknowledging his own prejudices, especially towards Roman Catholics:

> I acknowledged my lack of love towards others, especially towards professing Christians with whom I did not agree...I discovered vast numbers of true brothers and sisters in Christ whom I never knew existed.[34]

For Michael Green, this was important. He told me that:

> Another part of his legacy is an inclusive doctrine of the church which doesn't for a moment do away with the need for conversion, but does say that those who are Christ's really are my brothers and sisters—it doesn't matter how far 'up the candle' they are. And that cost him dear—a lot of people regarded him as very unsound for that.

Watson was widely criticized amongst evangelicals for his comment at the 1977 Nottingham Evangelical Anglican Conference (NEAC), where he said:

> In many ways, the Reformation was one of the greatest tragedies that ever happened to the church. Martin Luther...never wanted to split the church, simply to reform it.[35]

Indeed virtually every interviewee recalled Watson's NEAC speech, without the need for any specific prompting. Watson clearly caused a stir, particularly because most people read the press headlines, on 'The Tragedy of the Reformation' as a comment on doctrine rather than ecclesiology.

Despite the bad press, Watson continued to work hard for unity, especially between Protestants and Catholics in Northern Ireland and also amongst the divided church in South Africa.

This increasing appreciation of the breadth of the church was seen not just at Watson's festivals (where Christians were united in worship and evangelism) but also in the way he was able to integrate models from other traditions. For example, prior to Wimber, Watson learned about healing mainly from Anglo-Catholics, such as Maurice Maddocks, then Bishop of Selby, and saw a number of healings take place, especially in pastoral ministry in St Michael's Vicarage.

Today, the *Alpha* course is similarly transcending boundaries of tradition and denomination, and is presently receiving a warm welcome amongst Roman Catholics. As more and more local churches participate in *Alpha*, there can be a unifying and reconciliatory by-product. Nicky Gumbel picked up Watson's broad ecclesiology in our interview and, interestingly, linked it with *Alpha*:

> If you take a book like *The Household of God*, where Lesslie Newbigin talks about the three streams: the Catholic, the Protestant and the Pentecostal, you can see how David Watson was trying to work across that breadth, and that's what we (at *Alpha*) are trying to do. We believe that each of these is a move of God, although some people would dismiss one or other of them, or even all of them! But we feel that God is at work in the Catholic church and the Protestant church and in the Pentecostal church and that there are enormous strengths in all three of these movements, and that we need to learn from one another...

This theme of reconciliation between Christians in the UK has, to a large extent, been lost from the ecclesial agenda of evangelicals in the Church of England in recent years. The success of *Alpha* may have begun help to redress this issue.

Reconciliation, then, was a key theme for David Watson and an increasingly important one as he saw the need for forgiveness and unity before effective renewal and evangelism could take place.

6 Discipleship and the Future Church

We have seen that evangelism, renewal and reconciliation were the three main emphases of Watson's ministry.

They are still highly relevant for the future church, and are themes worth embracing by the emerging generation of church leaders who do not remember Watson and St Michael-le-Belfrey.

In fact, these three themes represent three important dimensions of church life: the *outward* (relationship with unbelievers—evangelism); the *upward* (relationship with God—renewal); the *inward* (relationship with other believers—reconciliation). These three dimensions of church life were modelled at St Michael's and to the wider church by Watson. They have been noted by missiologists and others concerned for a biblical and holistic structure for church vision, including US theologians Daniel Albrecht and Stanley Grenz, institutions such as Fuller Theological Seminary, which structures its programmes around this three-fold ministry emphasis, and churches in the UK such as St Thomas', Crookes, Sheffield. Watson may well be found to have made a significant contribution to the development of this three-fold vision.

Our analysis of Watson's influence on the future church should not, however, be confined to evangelism, renewal and reconciliation, because there were other relevant aspects to Watson that we have not yet discussed, most notably his lifestyle and character. In fact, Watson's ministry and life could be summarized under the theme of *Discipleship,* the title of both this chapter and one of his final books.

Discipleship and Materialism

Watson is at his most challenging and succinct on the issue of material wealth in *Discipleship.* He wrote:

> It is God's rebuke to us affluent Christians, as we hedge ourselves around with earthly treasures and securities, that God's power is today much more obviously demonstrated amongst those who have little or nothing of this world's goods. But they are rich in faith.[36]

Watson therefore modelled his convictions through the community house-holds and by seeking to live a simple lifestyle. He expressed it like this:

> For many of us, on both personal and corporate levels, there is an urgent need for a new image altogether, a radical discipleship mod-elled on the simplicity of Jesus, if we are to demonstrate with credibility the values of the kingdom of God.[37]

I asked a number of interviewees about the evangelical church's present at-titude to wealth, possessions and simple lifestyle. Most agreed that this was a key area of Watson's teaching that the church of the future must address. Graham Cray, speaking of the church's future need, put it like this:

> ...if we need *anything* it's the mutually supportive community that helps you live a life of simplicity in an increasingly consumer society. I actually think that if we need a David Watson book circulating it is probably *Discipleship* more than even *I Believe in Evangelism*. We don't have to try to recreate extended households and some of the other things we did, but there are serious issues about discipleship—in re-lation to identity and wealth and consuming and the poor.

Sue Hope also thinks that this is the main issue that the future church needs to hear from Watson:

> I think top of the list has to be materialism, and I say that to myself as well. I think it's probably the major inhibitory factor to evangelism in the west, and it acts like a blanket and dumbs the things down...

Despite Watson's commitment to a simple lifestyle, he nevertheless lived a busy and pressured life. He handled the pressure through hard work and by efficient organization. A number of my interviewees mentioned his notebook that he carried with him on all occasions, ready to record anything that might be of future use. In this regard, said John Collins, he was like John Stott:

> They both had that knack of every half hour of the day was organized. It didn't matter who was preaching, David had his notebook out and was taking notes. He was always learning. I think that was terrific.

There is much that future church leaders could learn from the example of David Watson. His efficient, meticulous manner and ruthless organization certainly helped his ministry.

Discipleship and Weaknesses

Watson's hard work was apparent to all who knew him although some thought he might have worked too hard. Watson's punishing work sched-ule could not be sustained forever. Sadly it was when he moved to London and was able to slow down a little, that his cancer was first diagnosed and within a year he was dead.

For David Hilborn this is an issue pertinent for Christian leaders:

> At one level, it's worrying that someone (like Watson) can reach that kind of position and still be living that way; on the other hand it's incredibly comforting and incredibly affirming—'hey, you know, I'm not unique, this is a common syndrome among evangelicals.' Theologically, there are big questions in that for me, particularly for a Protestant tradition that places so much emphasis on justification by faith alone and yet is so pragmatist and activist in its ministerial work.

A second area of weakness was in his leadership. In many ways his leadership style was exemplary, and people were won over by his charming personality, yet there were times when he was at one of two extremes. On some occasions he did not give a strong enough lead, and his biography and a number of interviewees suggest that he sometimes delegated too much authority to his elders. At other times, according to Rob Warner, Watson was too authoritarian. Inevitably, a man with such influence and gifting is vulnerable to misusing power. Indeed as a gifted leader he constantly faced the temptation of being 'a one-man-band' despite developing a large and skilled lay team for ministry at St Michael-le-Belfrey; this was because he was the best at most things—at preaching, at leading, at delivering the liturgy, at leading people to Christ. The result was that an attitude of complacency could and probably did develop at St Michael's the longer Watson was there.

Whilst he invested in his team, Watson did not stress the training or equipping of the wider church for ministry. This emphasis came more from Wimber in the 1980s. Perhaps Watson hoped to address this to some extent by establishing his 'Fuller in London'—which of course never came about. The practical training of both leaders and the wider church is a priority for the future church to be effective disciples and disciple-makers.

A third area of weakness, for which Watson could not be personally blamed, was his health. He suffered from both asthma and depression. Interestingly these were both a hindrance and a help to his ministry. They were a hindrance, in that he was unable to function at full strength for much of his ordained ministry. However, there were benefits. According to Cray:

> However radical and challenging what you'd heard had been, you came away feeling that if God could do it with someone who struggled the way David did, then God could do it for you.

Such honesty and vulnerability from such a church leader is commendable and reflects someone with a resilience of character.

Discipleship and Character

Virtually all those I interviewed spoke of Watson's integrity, kindness and compassion. Watson did not hide the fact that he suffered from depression or that his marriage was sometimes under strain. This naturally kept him from any triumphalism—which is probably one reason why he became the acceptable face of charismatic renewal in the 1970s and early 1980s.

Graham Cray, amongst others, talked of how he spoke out of honest experience in his preaching:

> …he shared himself in a way that enabled people to believe that what he was preaching about was something that God could help them to do.

In essence, Watson exemplified an *incarnational model* of ministry. This was especially noted by Martyn Percy—one often critical of charismatic evangelicalism:

> He was developing all the time a much more common, mainstream *lingua* that was bringing evangelical fundaments to a much wider audience, and he doesn't seem to be doing it for anyone's advantage other than yours and mine. And I think for me that's one of the really appealing things which comes over time and time again in his taped talks and books. You don't feel the drum is being banged for anybody; not for him; not for his party; but it's being banged for you. I mean, you can't praise that too highly. That is *so* gracious; *so* incarnational.

Discipleship—Conclusion

The greatest lesson of Watson's life is not for future generations to copy him, for he was a man of his time and imperfect like us all. However, the Spirit of God was able to use him more than most as he exemplified a life of character and integrity—seeking a truly incarnational approach to ministry. There is much for us to learn here. This is perhaps best summed up in a story describing an event in 1983—the year his body was battling with cancer. It was told to me by Diana Nairne:

> I had a most extraordinary experience—and this is a really *typical* experience of David. We went to this very very cold church and we were all very miserable and it was a grey November day and David's mouth was full of thrush and it was very uncomfortable. His back was hurting him because of the cancer and he was really feeling very rough. And one of the girls who was dancing was in a really cross mood because it was very cold and we had to dance in bare feet. And

also there wasn't a sprung floor—it was a stone floor. So to dance on that in the cold is not good. And she was very stroppy about it! And she stormed downstairs to the women's dressing room. And I was just going down and David came and said, 'Do you know where Ally is?' and I said, 'Yes actually, she's down stairs.' So I took him to the dressing room and he went in and he said, 'Ally, take off your leg-warmers' and we wondered what on earth he was going to do! And he just knelt down and he said, 'Put your foot here' and he just began to massage it and warm it up. And he did it quite vigorously and so it made him very out of breath—because he was also very asthmatic—and I just remember that both of us were really quite choked at this because we knew how rough he was feeling. And then at the end he just said 'Right, would you both pray for me, because I think I'm going to need your prayers just to get through this talk.'

Books by David Watson

Learning to Lead Group Bible Study (London: Falcon Press, 1962)

Towards Tomorrow's Church: A Practical Guide for Church-based Youth Club (London: Falcon Press, 1965).

My God is Real (Eastbourne: Kingsway, 1970)

Hidden Warfare (Bromley: Send the Light, 1970)

One in the Spirit (London: Hodder & Stoughton, 1973)

In Search of God (Eastbourne: Kingsway, 1974)

Live a New Life (Leicester: Inter-Varsity Press, 1975)

I Believe in Evangelism (London: Hodder & Stoughton, 1976)

I Believe in the Church (London: Hodder & Stoughton, 1978)

Is Anyone There? (London: Hodder & Stoughton, 1979)

Start a New Life (Eastbourne: Kingsway, 1979)

My Path of Prayer (Worthing: Henry E Walter, 1981)—chapter 9

Discipleship (London: Hodder & Stoughton, 1981)

Be Filled with the Spirit (Eastbourne: Kingsway, 1982)

Through the Year with David Watson (London: Hodder & Stoughton, 1982)

Jesus Then and Now (Tring: Lion, 1983) with Simon Jenkins

You are my God (London: Hodder & Stoughton, 1983)

Fear No Evil (London: Hodder & Stoughton, 1984)

Notes

1   T Saunders and H Samson, *David Watson—A Biography* (London: Hodder & Stoughton, 1992).

2   E J H Nash, known as 'Bash,' ran Christian camps for public school boys at Iwerne Minster.

3   After Gillingham, John Collins was Vicar at Canford Magna, Dorset and Holy Trinity Brompton, London. All his churches have experienced significant growth and become centres for charismatic renewal. According to Gavin Reid 'John Collins is the most unrecognized star person in the modern evangelical movement.'

4   For definitions and further analysis, see chapter 4.

5   *Fear No Evil*, p 56. This writer remembers hearing Wimber speak in the early 1990s and describing Watson's body bouncing up and down on the bed as they prayed for him.

6   *I Believe in the Church*, p 298.

7   *ibid*, p 300.

8   *ibid*, p 301.

9   *ibid*, pp 134-5.

10 R Warren, *Building Missionary Congregations* (London: Church House Publishing, 1995) p 2.

11 After citing numerous statistics to build his case, the historian Adrian Hastings writes: 'It is not exaggerated to conclude that between 1960 and 1985 the Church of England as a going concern was effectively reduced to not much more than half its previous size.' *A History of English Christianity, 1920-1990* (London: SCM, 1986, 1987, 1991) p 603.

12 *I Believe in Evangelism*, p 24.

13 H Rookmaaker, *Modern Art and the Death of a Culture* (London: IVF, 1970).

14 *ibid*, pp 9, 41.

15 *I Believe in Evangelism*, p 166.

16 D Bebbington, *Evangelicalism in Modern Britain* (Grand Rapids: Baker, 1989) p 244.

17 This was brought home particularly in the research written up in J Finney, *Finding Faith Today* (Swindon: Bible Society, 1992) chapter 3.

18 A model developed by James F Engel showing a scale of receptiveness to the gospel. It begins at minus 10 (awareness of the supernatural) and progresses to minus 1 (repentance and faith) before positive numbers are reached (for example, initiation into church).

19 In places they use identical quotes, share the same illustrations, and use virtually the same points in making key doctrinal statements. Chapters can begin similarly and there are a few passages that may have been borrowed or re-written.

20 *I Believe in the Church,* p 170.

21 In 1963 Watson was forced to leave his lodgings at the evangelical institution, Tyndale House, because 'the authorities there heard he had used tongues privately in his prayers' (Saunders, *op cit,* p 82).

22 *You are My God,* p 56.

23 *ibid.*

24 *Third Wave* was a term coined by missiologist Peter Wagner to describe what he saw as a new (3rd) wave of the Spirit in the 20th Century—the first wave being Pentecostalism and the second charismatic renewal.

25 London: Hodder & Stoughton, 1985 and 1986 respectively .

26 'Worship and Unity' Conference at Holy Trinity Brompton 1994, tape 2. It is likely that he was keen to make contacts in the UK and Wimber must soon have became aware, after meeting Watson, that he was one of the best connected Christians in all of Britain.

27 Wimber's UK ministry actually began at St Andrew's Chorleywood, led by David Pytches. Pytches had wanted to invite Wimber to the UK, and hearing he was coming to York arranged for him to visit on the way north.

28 *The Essence of Discipleship*—tape 4—Conference at Holy Trinity Brompton's Focus Holiday, Summer 1995.

29 This was exactly the dilemma the Anglican Church faced in the 18th Century with John Wesley, who saw the world as his parish.

30 M Harper, 'The Reconciler' in E England, *A Portrait By His Friends* p 57.

31 *ibid,* p 155.

32 'The Toronto Blessing' is the name given to a particular charismatic experience that originated in the Toronto Airport Vineyard Church in 1994. Particular phenomena associated with this experience include falling, shaking, laughing and occasionally the making of animal noises.

33 *You Are My God,* p 184.

34 *ibid,* p 99.

35 *ibid,* p 102.

36 *Discipleship,* p 219.

37 *ibid,* p 211.